Six Steps to Professional Success

CV WRITING WORKBOOK

Gwyneth Letherbarrow

Feelgood Coaching and Consulting

CONTENTS

FOREWORD i

STEP ONE – THE CAREER COMPASS 1

STEP TWO - WHERE SHOULD YOU LOOK FOR YOUR JOB? 10

STEP THREE – WHO ARE YOU? 15

STEP FOUR – GATHERING THE FACTS 17

STEP FIVE - PAINT YOUR PICTURE 26

STEP SIX – BRINGING IT ALL TOGETHER 28

FOREWORD

At the end of 2012 I was holding a CV writing and interview skills workshop, and one of the participants told me that he was very worried about his future. The company he was working for was down-sizing, and because he was one of several people doing the same job, he was going to have to re-apply for his own position. He was convinced that another colleague was going to get the job because they got on with the boss better than he did, and he seemed close to despair. He worked hard at the workshop but I could see that he still had a lot of questions that only he could find the answers to, about himself, and about his employer.

Some six months later when I was holding more workshops at the same company, I received a message that a young man had asked to talk to me. It was the coffee break so I went to find him. At first I didn't recognize the confident, smiling face. "I got the job", he said, "thank you for changing my life". I was amazed, and overjoyed. This was the same young man who had previously seemed so close to giving up on himself. He told me that he had taken everything on board from the workshops, and had worked hard at rebranding himself.

There is no magic wand that I can wave and make everything alright for you. It's YOU that has to take action. But what I can promise you is that if you commit to making sure that your application is relevant to each and every position for which you apply, you will have significantly increased the likelihood of your being called for interview.

Book Bonus – To receive one free review of your CV, sign up to my mailing list at: http://www.feelgoodcoachingandconsulting.com/#!career-coaching/cx3

www.feelgoodcoachingandconsulting.com

STEP ONE – THE CAREER COMPASS

"Begin with the end in mind" – Stephen Covey

If you don't know what you want, you won't ever get it. Start off by writing a list of everything you love to do. Think back to when you were a child. Did you love to dance, or read books, or play in the garden? What was it about those activities that made them fun? What do you enjoy doing now? What do other people tell you you're good at, even if it seems so easy to you that it doesn't seem important?

EXERCISE 1

I LOVE:

_____

_____

_____

_____

_____

_____

_____

_____

_____

_____

EXERCISE 2

Write down EVERYTHING that your dream job would include. What size of company are you going to work for? Is it in the private or public sector? What are you doing? How far do you have to travel (if at all)? What is your salary? How many hours do you work? How much holiday do you have? What other benefits are there – health insurance, discounts on products and services? BRAINSTORM and DARE TO DREAM because it's free !

_____

_____

_____

_____

_____

_____

_____

_____

_____

_____

_____

_____

_____

_____

EXERCISE 3

Your two lists from Exercises 1 and 2 will already have given you a better idea of the direction you want to go in. You now need to put your list in order of priority so that when you start your job search you know where areas of potential compromise might be (or not).

There are a couple of ways that you can do this, the first being what I call the 'Career Compass'.

Choose the eight most important elements of your dream job from your two lists. Put one element into each of the sections in the circle below. On a scale of zero to 10, how important is that element of your dream job? Give a score for each segment of the circle (zero is in the middle and 10 is at the edge of the circle). For example if the amount of holiday you get is really important to you, then you might decide to give it a '9', and if you would quite like to have regular working hours, but are prepared to compromise if it means having a higher salary you might give that section a '6'.

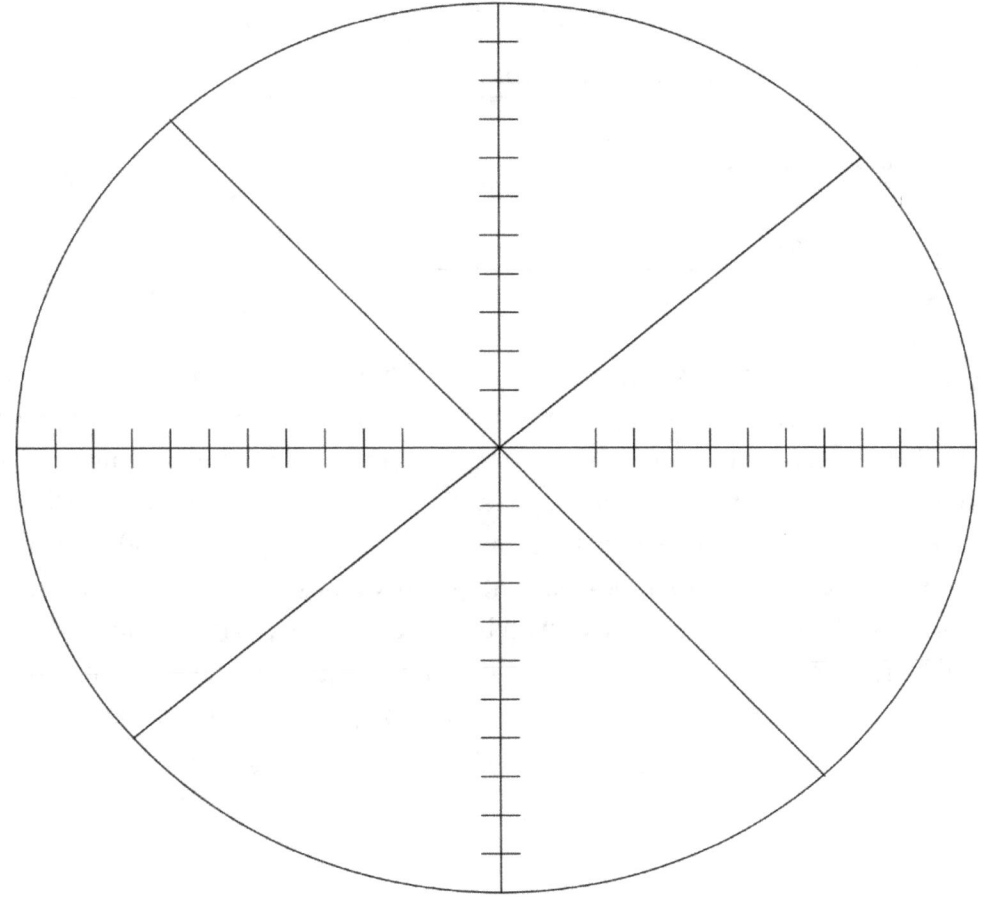

The second model might take a while longer but is well worth the effort (I learned this way of making choices from a very clever and successful Coach).

Say for example you had the following list (although yours is going to be much longer because you will have included everything from Exercises 1 and 2):

I want to work for a small company	
I want to earn EUR 2000 per month	X
I want to work 30 hours per month	X
I love talking to people	
I love cooking and food	
I want to travel a maximum of 15 minutes to work	
I want private health insurance	
I love spending time outside	

Start off by comparing the first two items on your list. Which of those two are more important to you? Put a cross or a tick next to the item that you choose. So for me it would be more important to earn EUR 2000 per month than to work for a small company. Then compare number one with number three and put a tick or a cross next to the statement that is more important. Having to decide between boxes one and three, my choice would be box three, to work 30 hours per month. Then compare box one with box four, box one with box five, box one with box six, and so on. Then you start again by comparing box two with box three, box two with box four, box two with box five … then move to box three and compare it with box four, box three with box five … then move to box four and compare it with box five … keep going until you have worked your way through the entire list, always marking the statement that is more important.

My example ends up looking like this:

1.	I want to work for a small company	
2.	I want to earn EUR 2000 per month	X X X X
3.	I want to work 30 hours per month	X X X X
4.	I love talking to people	X X X X X X
5.	I love cooking and food	X X X X X X X
6.	I want to travel a maximum of 15 minutes to work	X
7.	I want private health insurance	X X X X
8.	I love spending time outside	X X

What I have learned from this is that although I thought that working for a small company was quite important to me, in comparison to the other things I want, it has become completely irrelevant. I have also learned that I would probably be happy to have a longer journey to work if the other things I wanted were in place.

Now it's your turn. Put all your statements into the following table – add more pieces of paper if necessary. By the time you have finished you will be able to see the most important elements of the job that you LOVE and you will know what to look for when looking at vacancy notices.

1.		
2.		
3.		
4.		
5.		
6.		
7.		
8.		
9.		
10.		
11.		
12.		
13.		
14.		
15.		
16.		
17.		

EXERCISE 4

Have you ever labelled yourself with a job title, for example secretary, or solicitor, or marketer, or manager? That isn't who you are. If you met Richard Branson or Oprah Winfrey in the elevator and had 30 seconds to describe yourself, what would you say?

_____

_____

_____

_____

_____

_____

> "Your work is going to fill a large part of your life, and the only way to be truly satisfied is to do what you believe is great work. The only way to do great work is to LOVE what you do." *Steve Jobs*

NOTES

STEP TWO - WHERE SHOULD YOU LOOK FOR YOUR JOB?

"If opportunity doesn't knock, build a door." – Milton Berle

If you hear of someone having been 'headhunted' or offered a job, it's probably because someone told someone else who told someone else that they did their job really well. When did you last do some networking?

Believe it or not, one under-utilised way of looking for a job is via the internet. In addition to searching the websites of individual companies, you could also:
- Enter the title of the job you want and the town (or country) where you want to work in your internet search engine. You might be amazed at what comes up;
- Upload your CV onto LinkedIn;
- Upload your CV onto one of the many recruitment websites (although take care to find out whether they want to charge you).

Where else could you look? Newspapers or specialised magazines?

EXERCISE 5

Write down all your ideas.

_____

_____

_____

_____

_____

Who do you know who does something that you would love to do? Who could you tell that you are looking for a job? What are you going to tell them?

_____

_____

_____

_____

Move out of your comfort zone! What's the worst thing that could happen to you if you dared to dream, to do something new or different? Put another way, what will you be feeling or thinking next year or in five years' time if you don't take action now?

_____

_____

_____

_____

EXERCISE 6

Create your very own marketing plan. Imagine you were going to be launching a brilliant new product that people had been waiting to buy for months. What are the steps that you need to take?

Activity	Start Date	Planned End Date	Done
For example: Set up LinkedIn Profile	20/11	22/11	
Join three LinkedIn groups	1/12	1/12	

Activity	Start Date	Planned End Date	Done

NOTES

www.feelgoodcoachingandconsulting.com

STEP THREE – WHO ARE YOU?

"What lies before us and what lies behind us are very little compared to what lies within us" – Ralph Waldo Emerson

Your CV is your very own form of marketing, and like it or not, you have to 'sell' yourself to potential employers. What is your brand? How do you want other people to see you? What are your strengths? What is unique about you?

EXERCISE 7

My brand is:

_____

_____

_____

_____

_____

_____

_____

_____

_____

_____

NOTES

STEP FOUR – GATHERING THE FACTS

"Get your facts first, then you can distort them as you please." – Mark Twain

Your next step is to pull all your content together.

EXERCISE 8

Complete all the following information:

Your name: _____

Telephone _____

Email address: _____

Skype: _____

YOUR PROFILE (look back to Exercises 4 and 7)
How are you going to describe yourself?

_____

_____

_____

_____

Career history

State the names and addresses of previous employers (if applicable), and your dates of employment in reverse chronological order (ie., include the most recent first). What examples can you use to describe your activities?

Most recent job/dates _____

What did you do?   _____

                        _____

                        _____

                        _____

What did you do well?   _____

                        _____

                        _____

Next job and dates _____

What did you do?   _____

                        _____

                        _____

                        _____

What did you do well?   _____

                        _____

Next job and dates _____

What did you do?   _____

                               _____

                               _____

                               _____

What did you do well?   _____

                               _____

Next job and dates _____

What did you do?   _____

                               _____

                               _____

                               _____

What did you do well?   _____

NOTES

Education

List the details of university or college courses including the grade achieved, and your dates of study. Include the most recent first.

University (if applicable) _____

Dates and Grade(s) _____

Subject(s) studied _____

College (if applicable) _____

Dates and Grade(s) _____

Subject(s) studied _____

High School (if applicable) _____

Dates and Grade(s) _____

Subject(s) studied _____

Secondary/comprehensive school (if applicable) _____

Dates and Grade(s) _____

Subject(s) studied _____

Professional membership

If you are in the medical profession you may belong to the Medical Council, or if you work in finance you may belong to one of the Chartered Institutes.

_____

_____

Training and development

Make a list of all the courses you have studied which were not a part of your formal education, for example IT packages. If you have attended a lot of training courses ensure that you only include details about those that are relevant to each job application.

_____

_____

_____

_____

_____

Publications

This will usually be more relevant to positions requiring very specific qualifications in the medical, legal or educational sectors.

_____

_____

_____

Voluntary work

Have you taken part in any activities to support and help others?

_____

_____

_____

_____

Other information

Driving license and type   _____

Languages   _____

Software packages   _____

Hobbies   _____

Anything else?   _____

                            _____

Referees

You must ask permission from the person you wish to use as a referee. Who could you ask? Are they familiar with your work experience, academic qualifications or character? Most employers will ask for three referees, but you might want to ask four or five people when you start your job search so that you can select those that can provide information that is relevant for the job in question. Put their names and contact details here:

Referee 1 _____

_____

Referee 2 _____

_____

Referee 3 _____

_____

Referee 4 _____

_____

NOTES

STEP FIVE - PAINT YOUR PICTURE

**"Data! Data! Data!" he cried impatiently.
"I can't make bricks without clay." – Sherlock Holmes**

You have created an excellent basis for your application. Another way in which you can grab the attention of employers (and the software programmes that make an initial selection) is to use/match key words from the job vacancy notice in your application. You will have to do this for each position. Do not be tempted to send the same CV or Resumé for different jobs …

EXERCISE 9

Vacancy 1. _____

Keywords _____

Vacancy 2. _____

Keywords _____

Vacancy 3. _____

Keywords _____

Vacancy 4. _____

Keywords _____

Vacancy 5. _____

Keywords _____

NOTES

STEP SIX – BRINGING IT ALL TOGETHER

"Do your little bit of good where you are; it's those little bits of good put together that overwhelm the world." – Desmond Tutu

You have everything you need on the previous pages to put together a fabulous job application.

Keep it simple! Boxes, lines and lots of colours can be irritating on the eye, and your application must be easy to read. Clear headings such as those on the next page will help the person reading your CV to easily identify the information they need for a first selection.

> "You have brains in your head
> You have feet in your shoes
> You can steer yourself
> Any direction you choose"
> *Dr Seuss*

SIMPLE TEMPLATE FOR A CURRICULUM VITAE (CV) OR RESUMÉ

NAME
Telephone number/Skype
Email address

PROFILE

PROFESSIONAL EXPERIENCE

EDUCATION

OTHER TRAINING

OTHER INFORMATION

NOTES

RECORD OF JOB APPLICATIONS

Job title	Company	Date applied	Answer received	Interview Date

www.ingramcontent.com/pod-product-compliance
Lightning Source LLC
Chambersburg PA
CBHW081804170526
45167CB00008B/3323